I0488551

Inside the pages of this book you will find a variety of 30 different coloring illustrations of flower arrangements in vases for your creativity and relaxation.

If you enjoyed this book why not share your creations on our Facebook page below. Here you can also find more FREE coloring illustrations and patterns to copy.

https://www.facebook.com/Best-Adult-Coloring-Books-1497039227284351

Why not also check out my other books below.
Also available on Amazon

In The Zone: The Ultimate Stress Relief Colouring Book

Vintage Fairies And Angels Colouring Book: A Collection Of Vintage Illustrations To Colour

The Instant Relaxation Colouring Book: Powerful Mystic Mandalas For Mind Body & Spirit

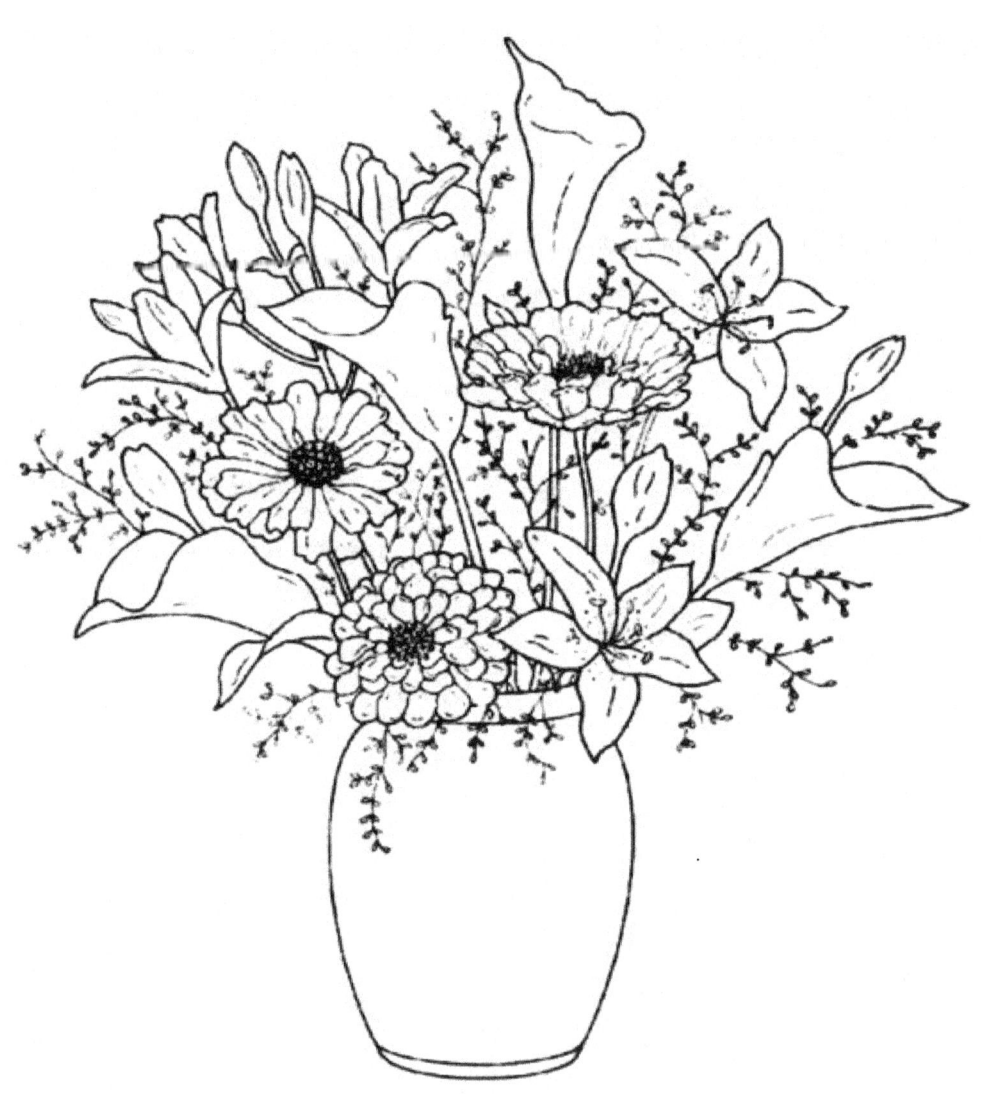

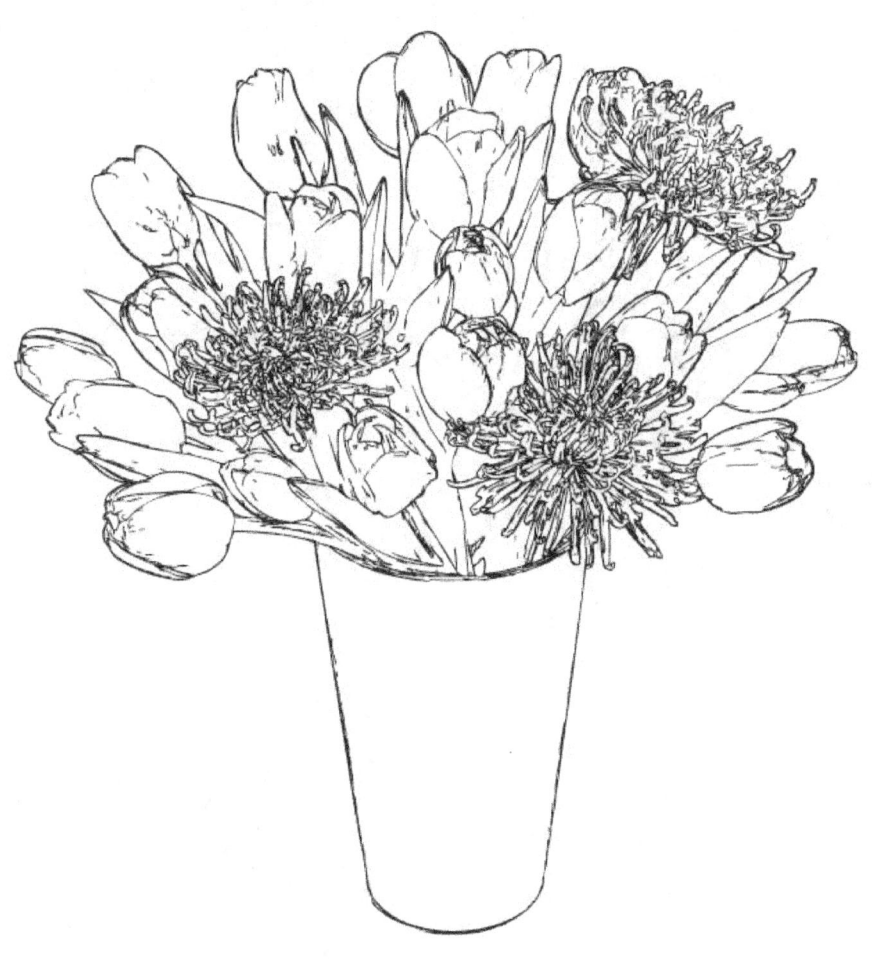

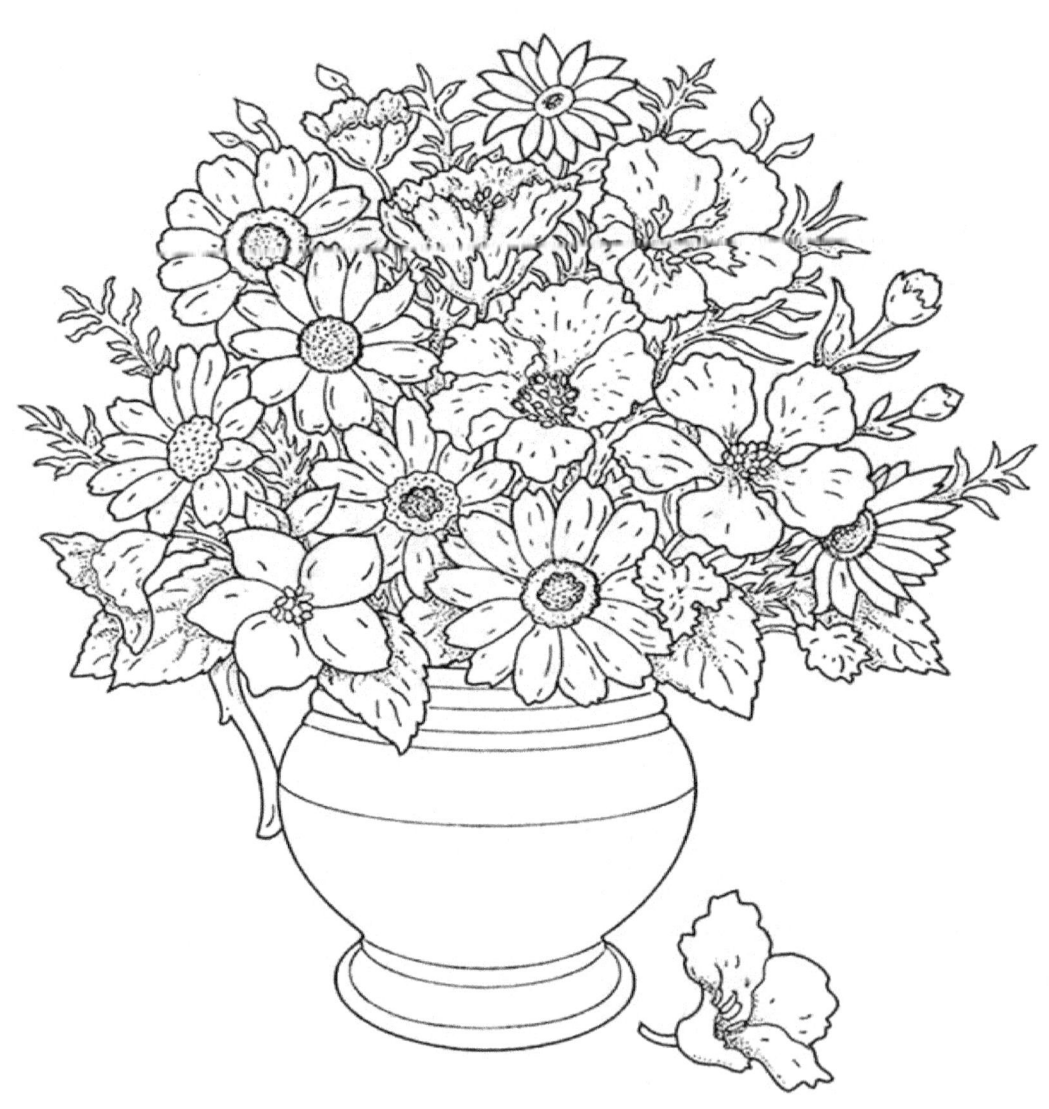

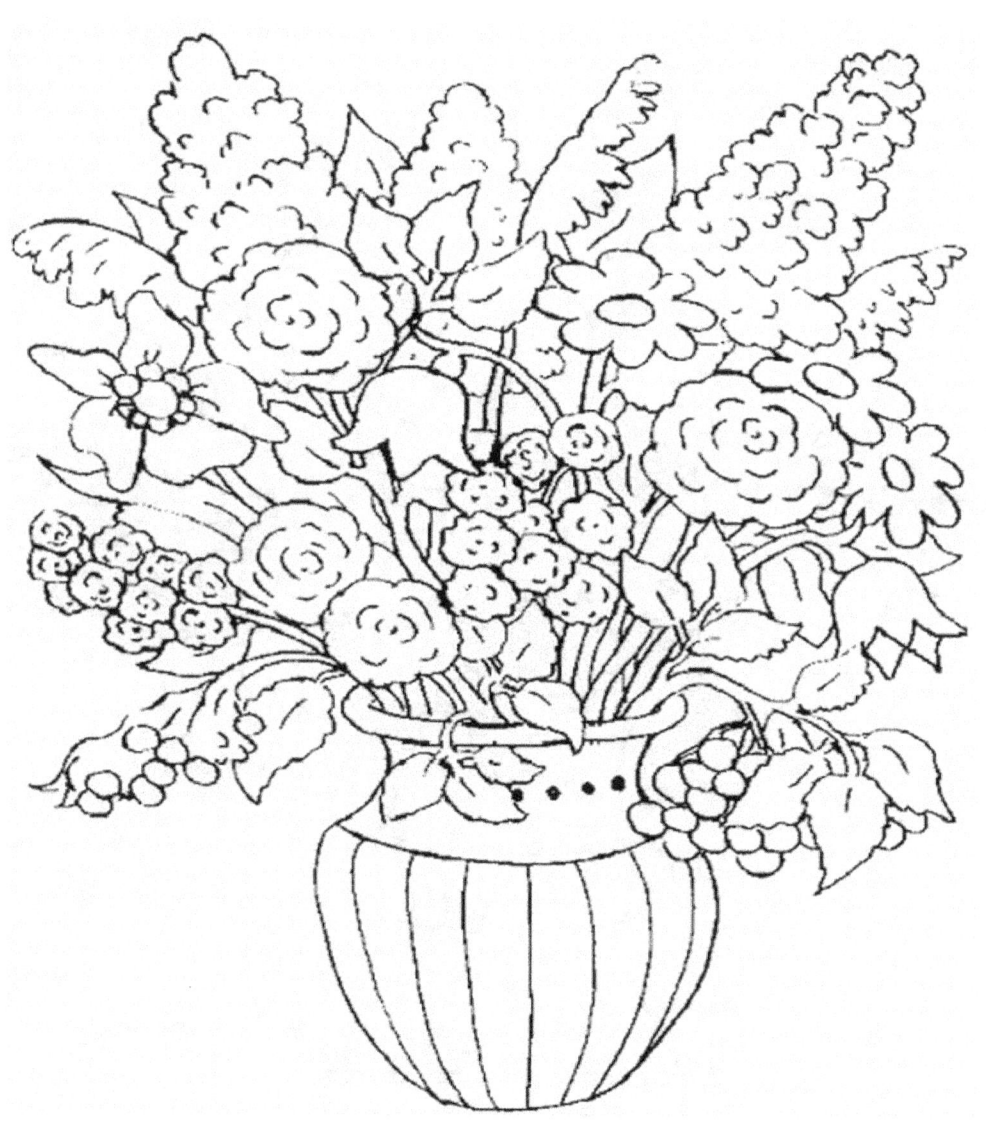

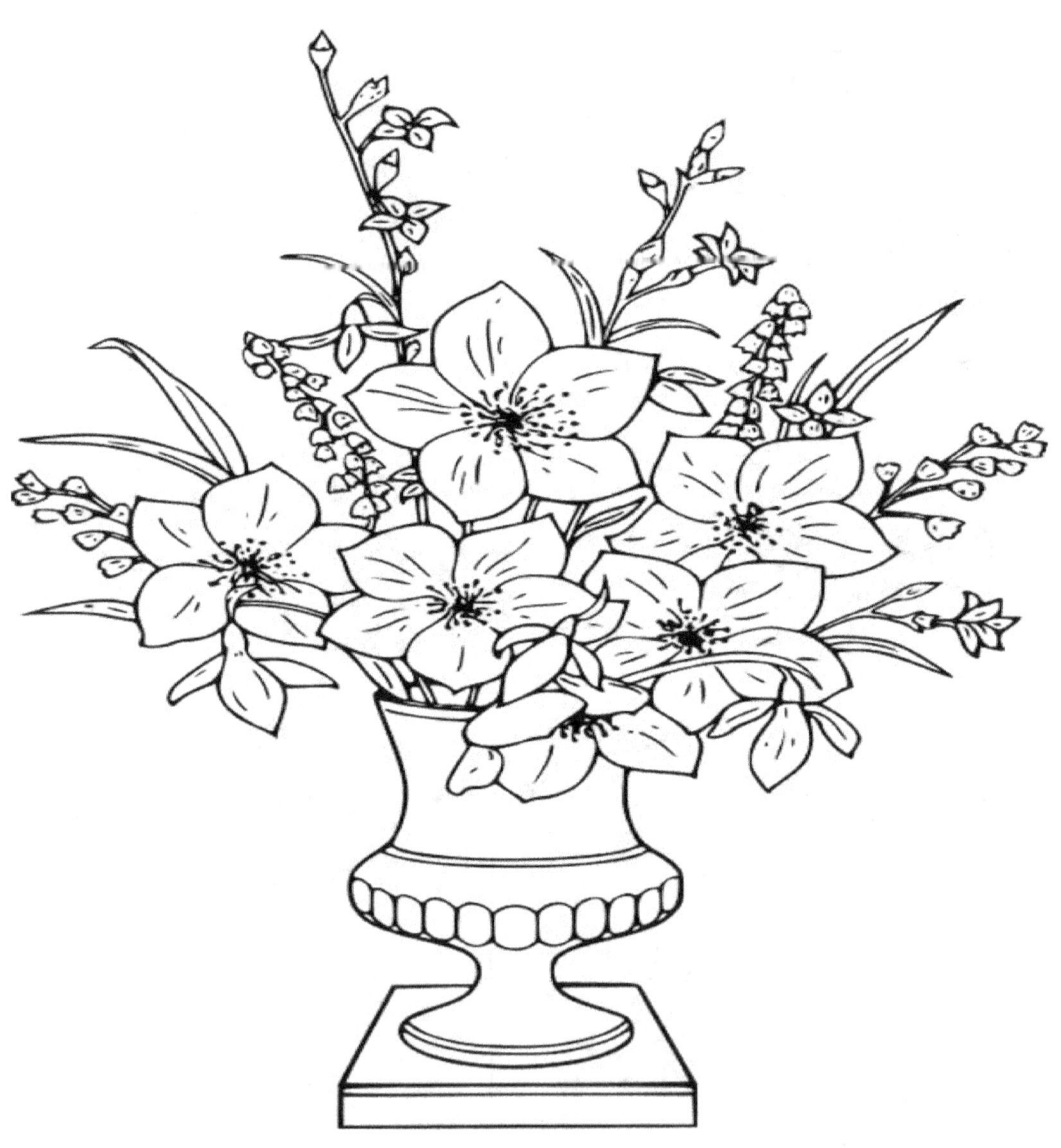

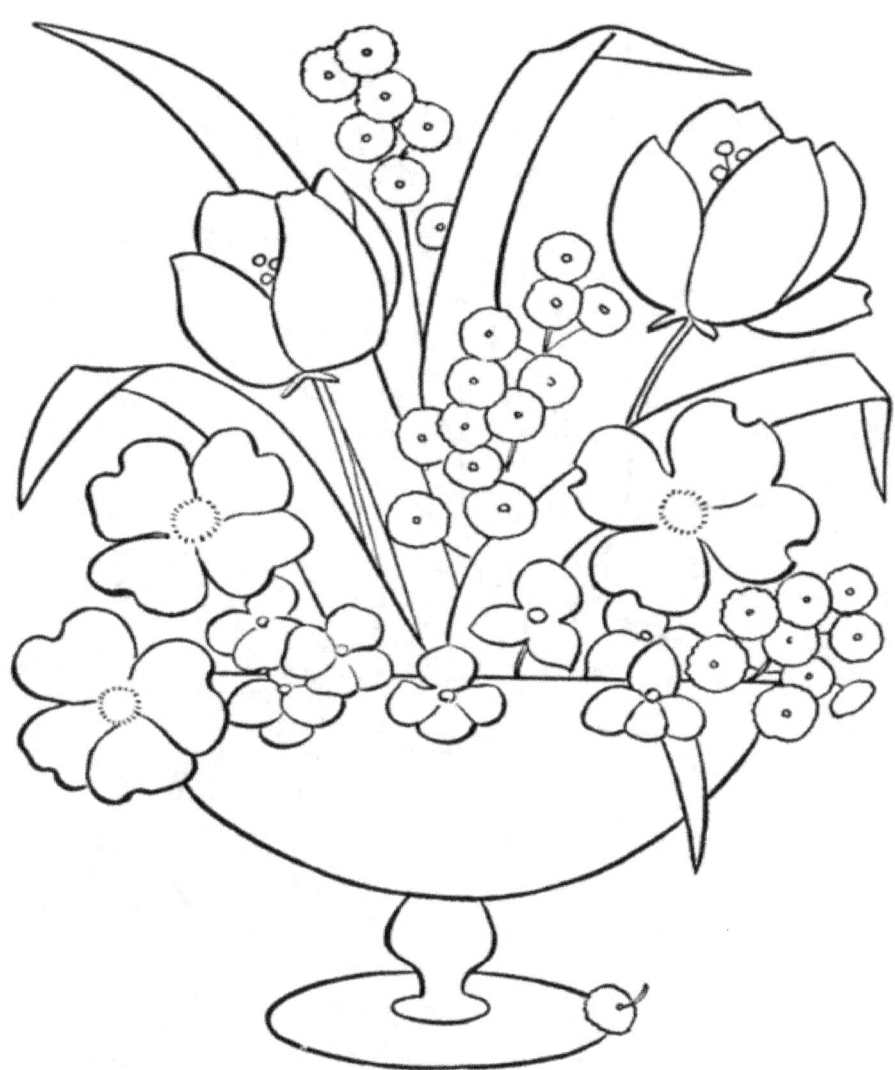

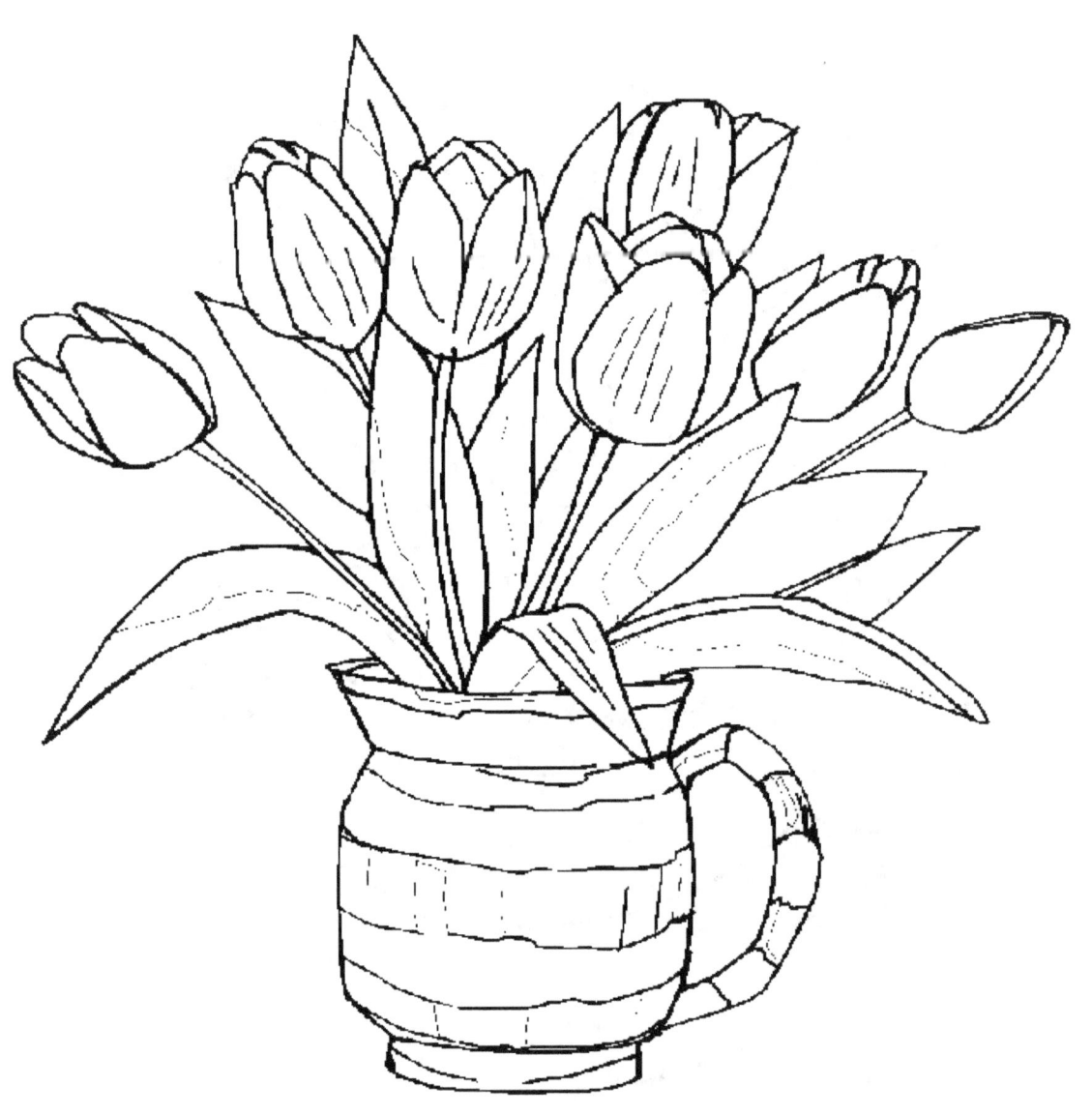

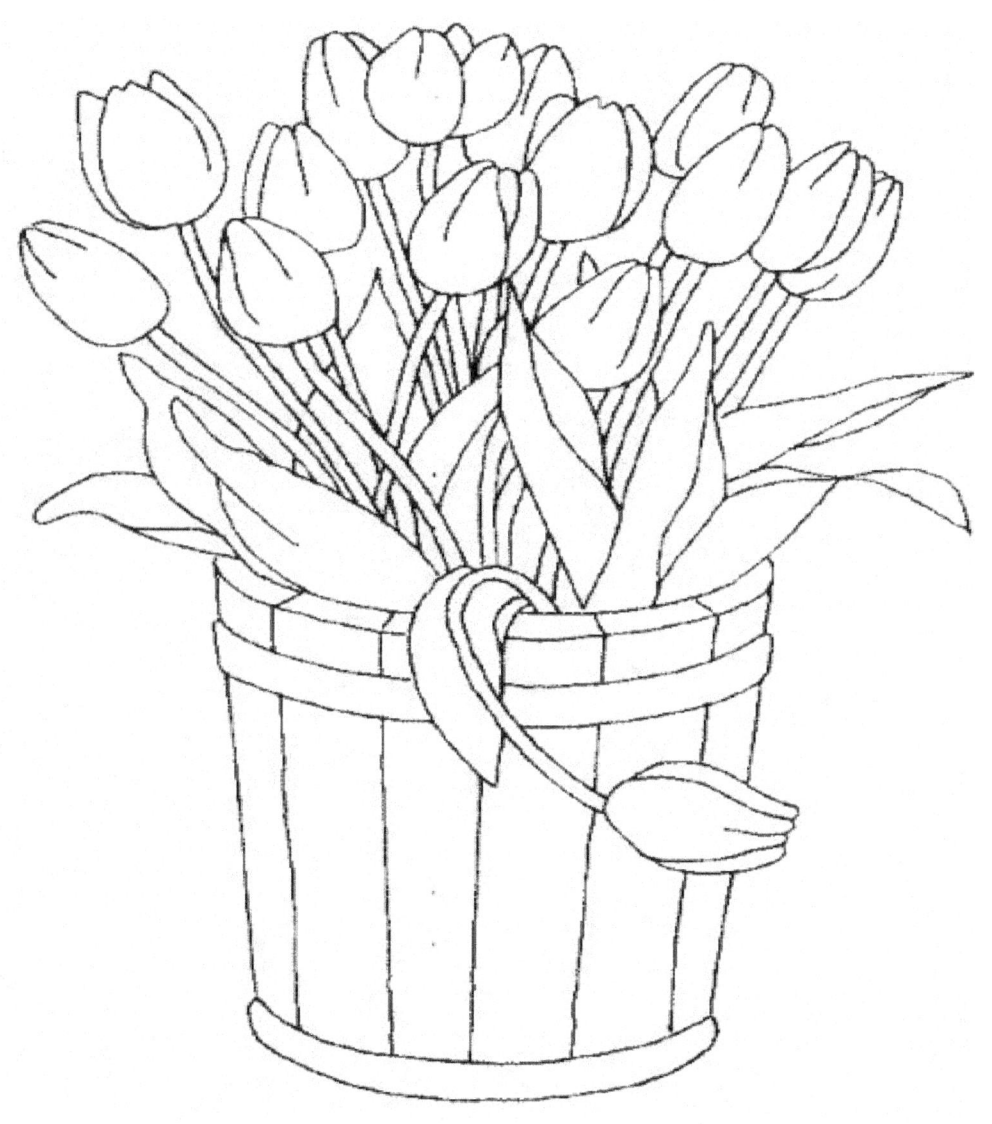

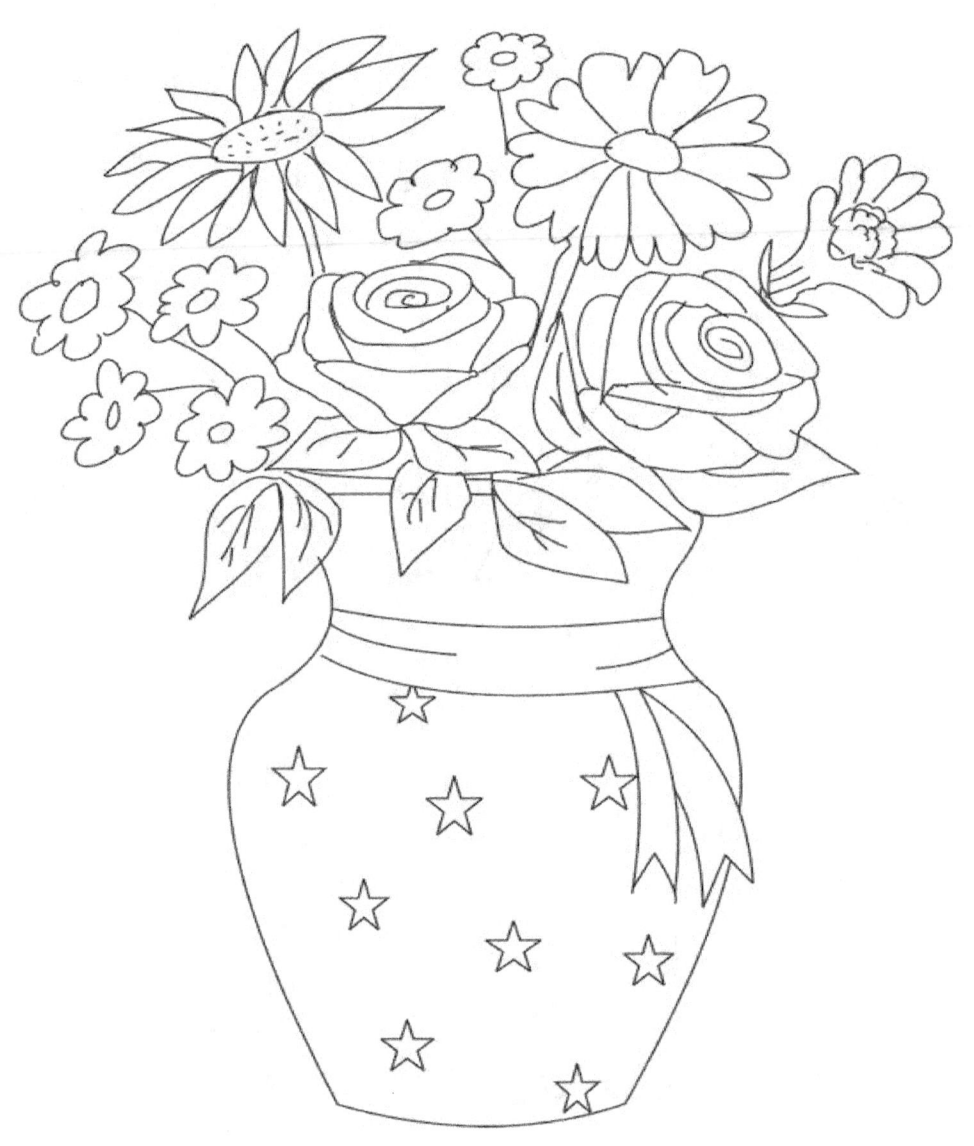

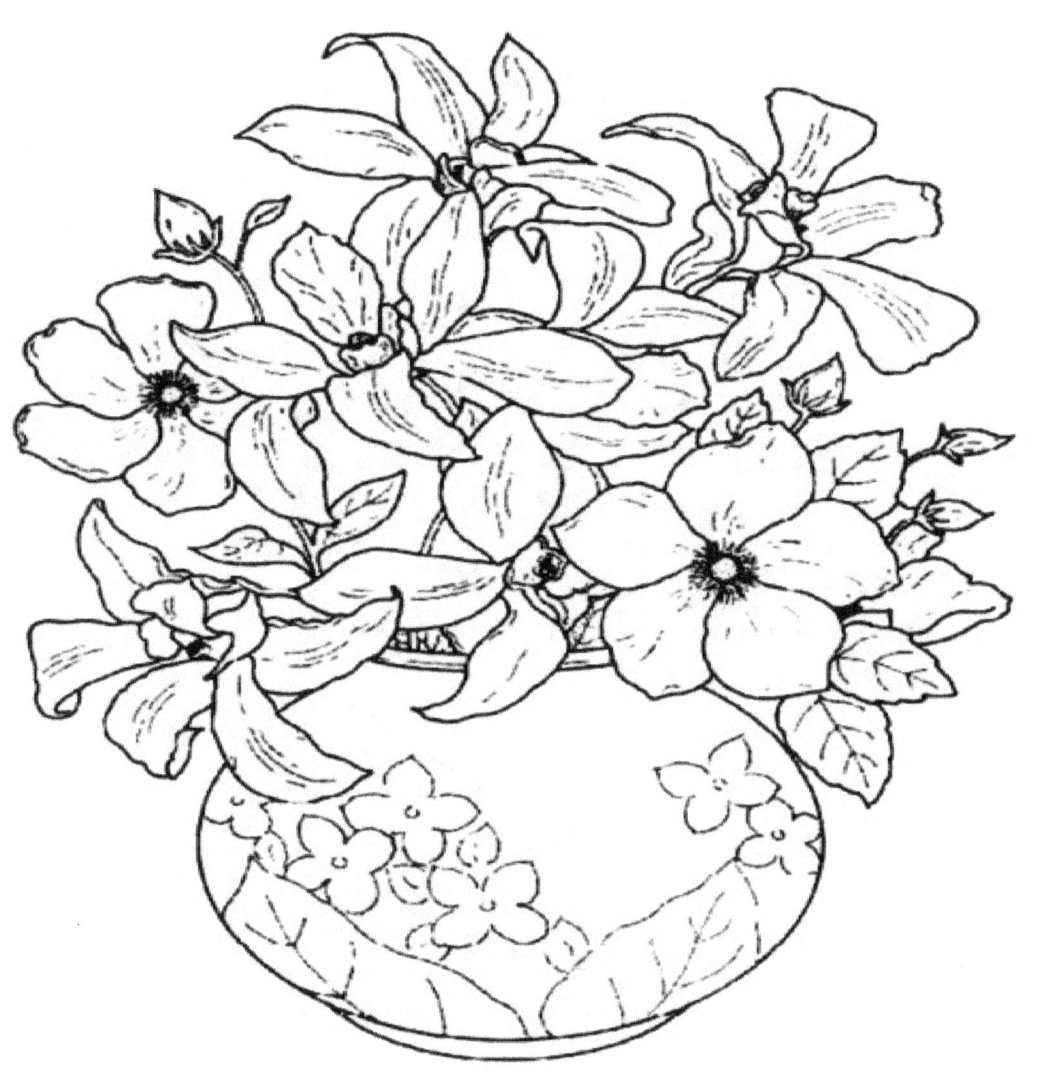

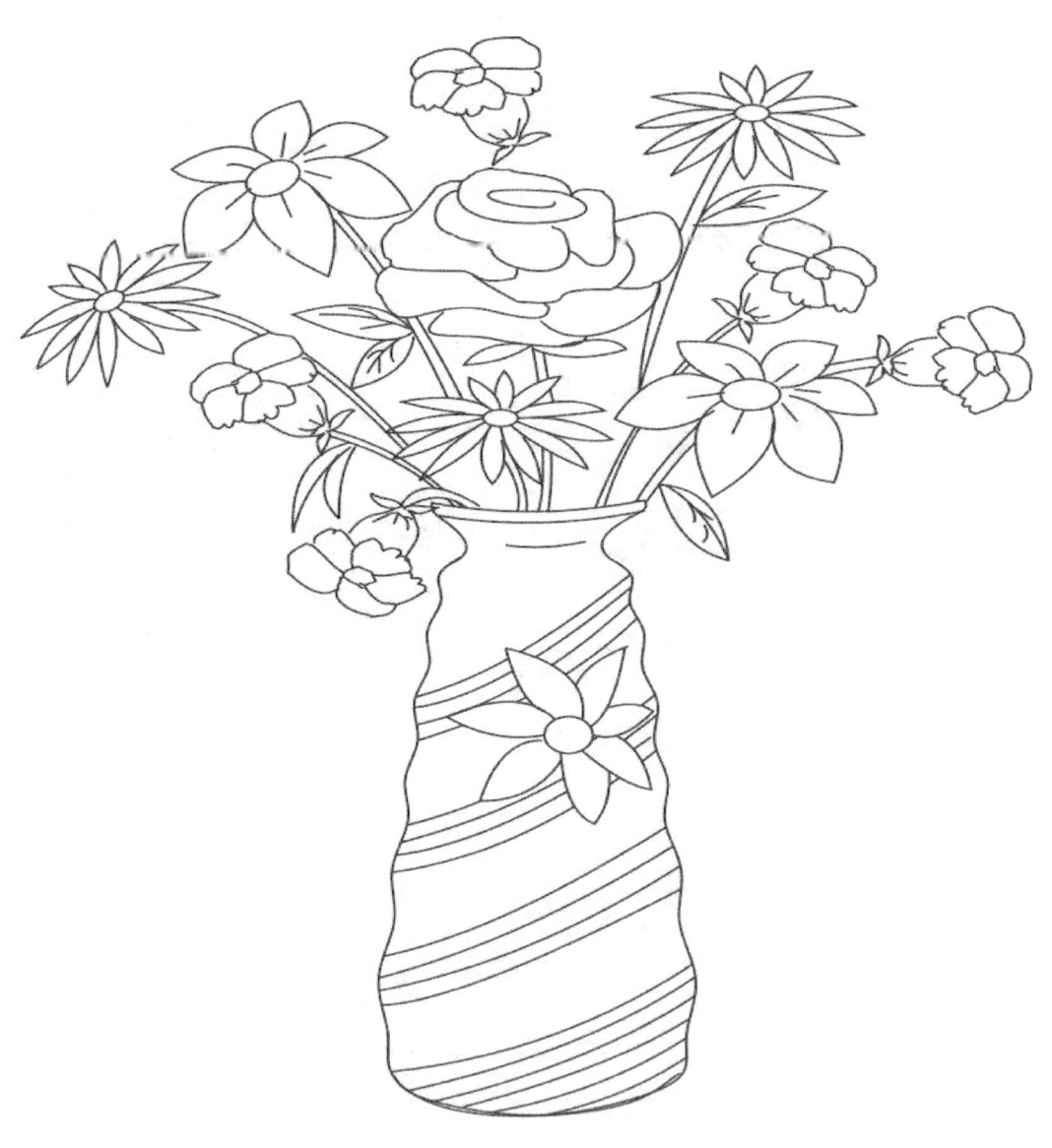

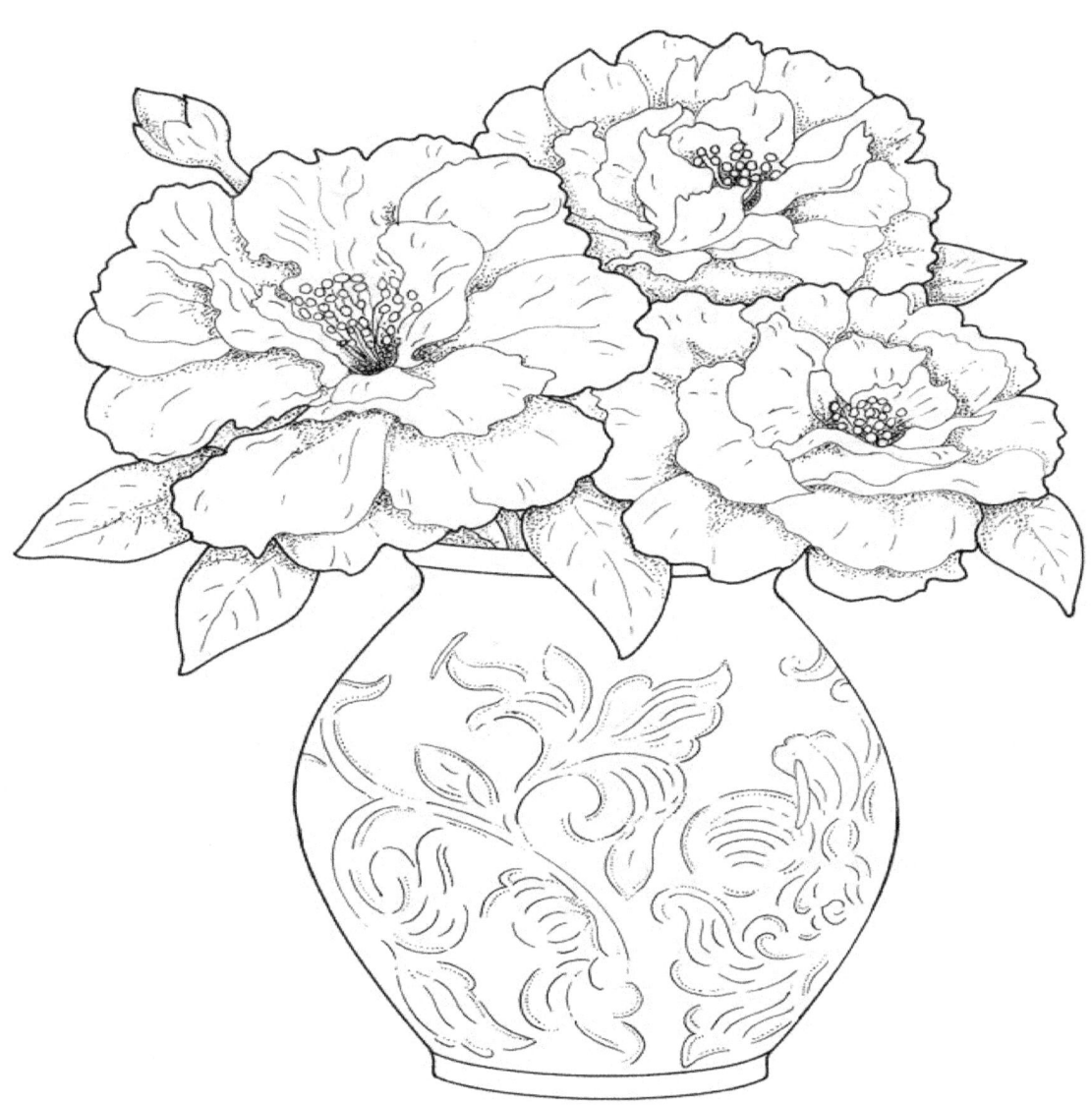

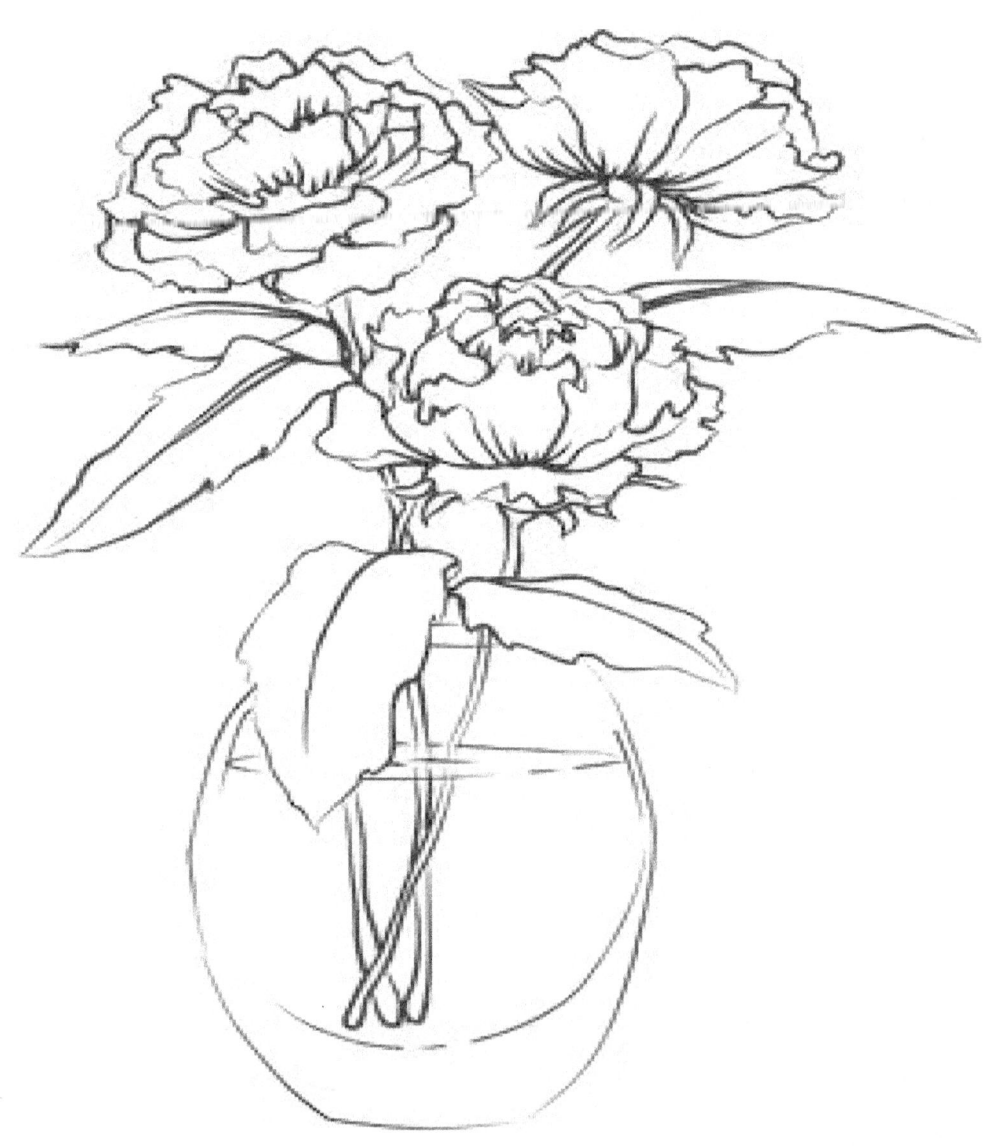

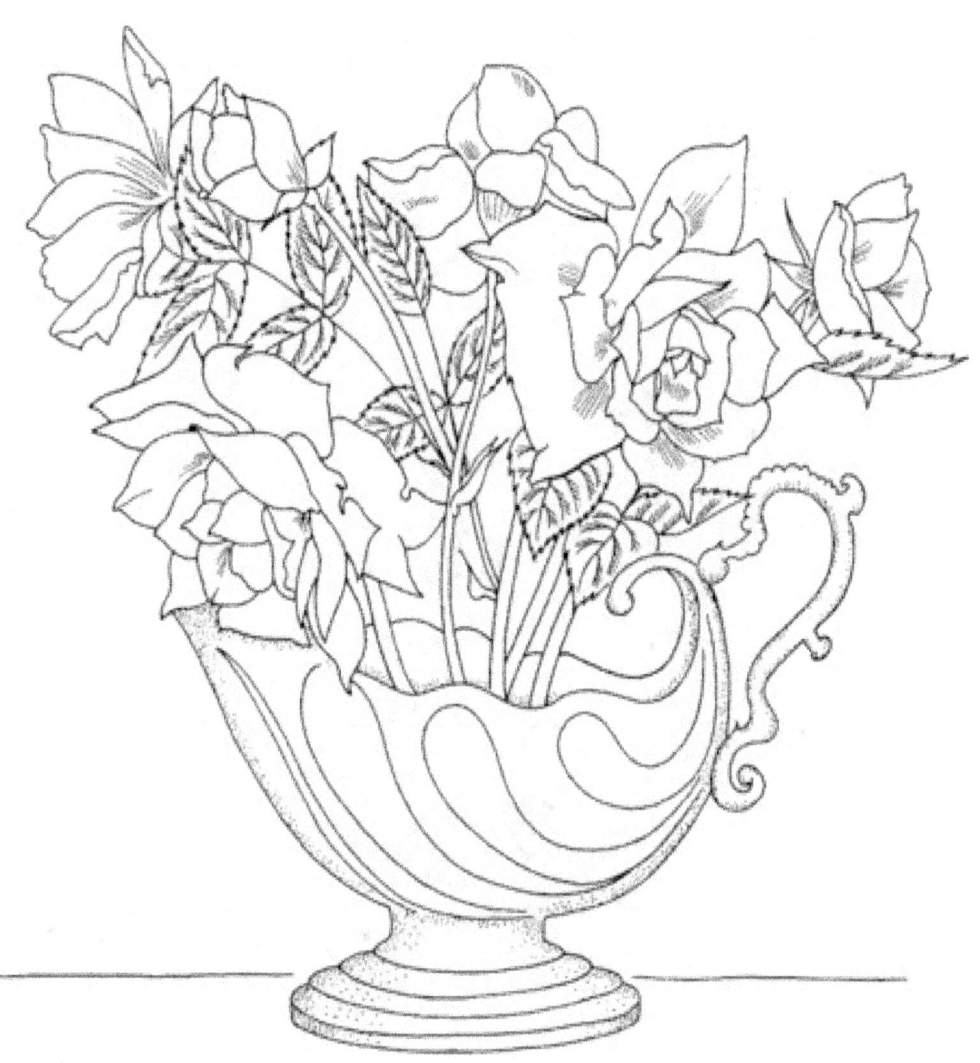

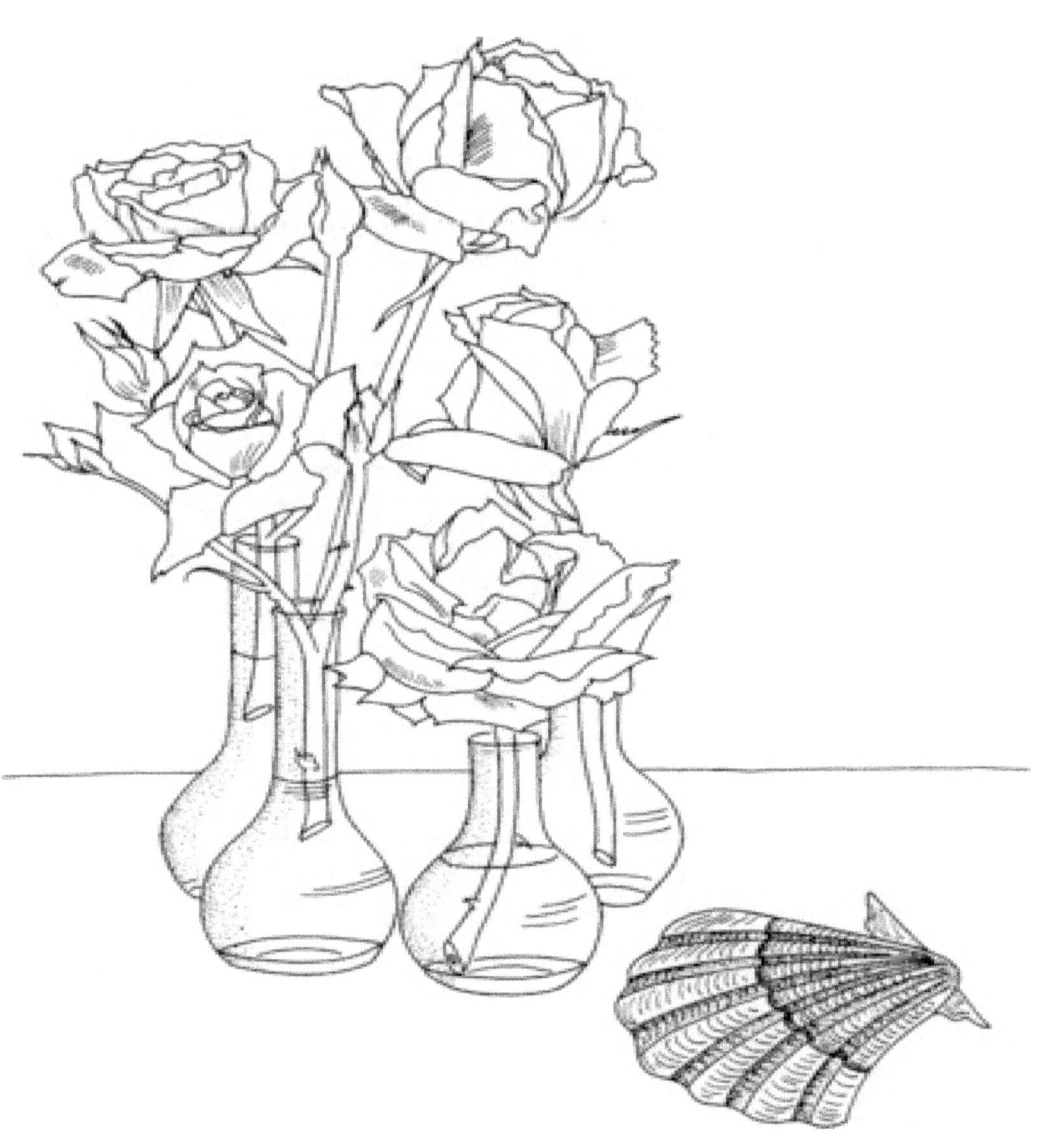

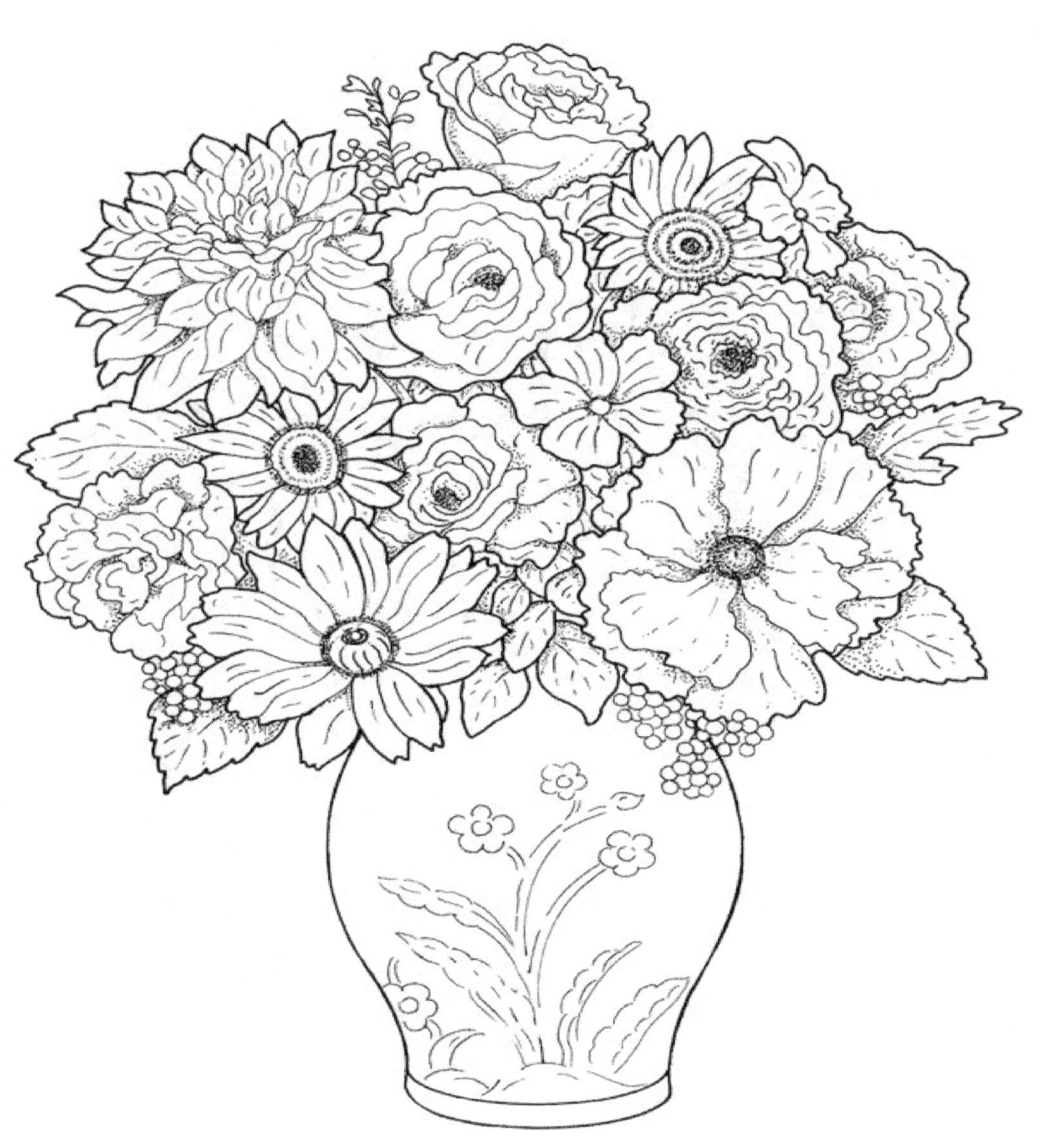

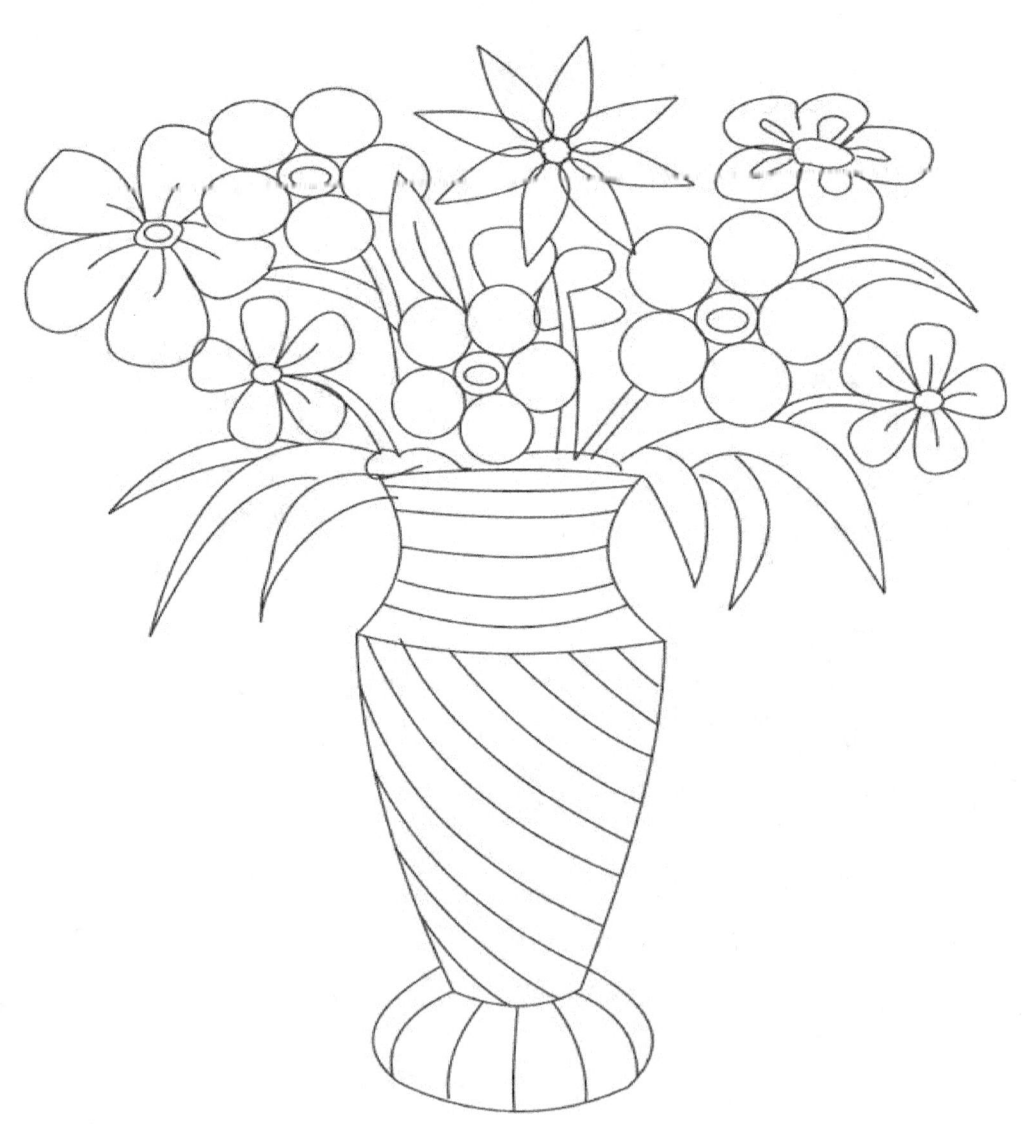

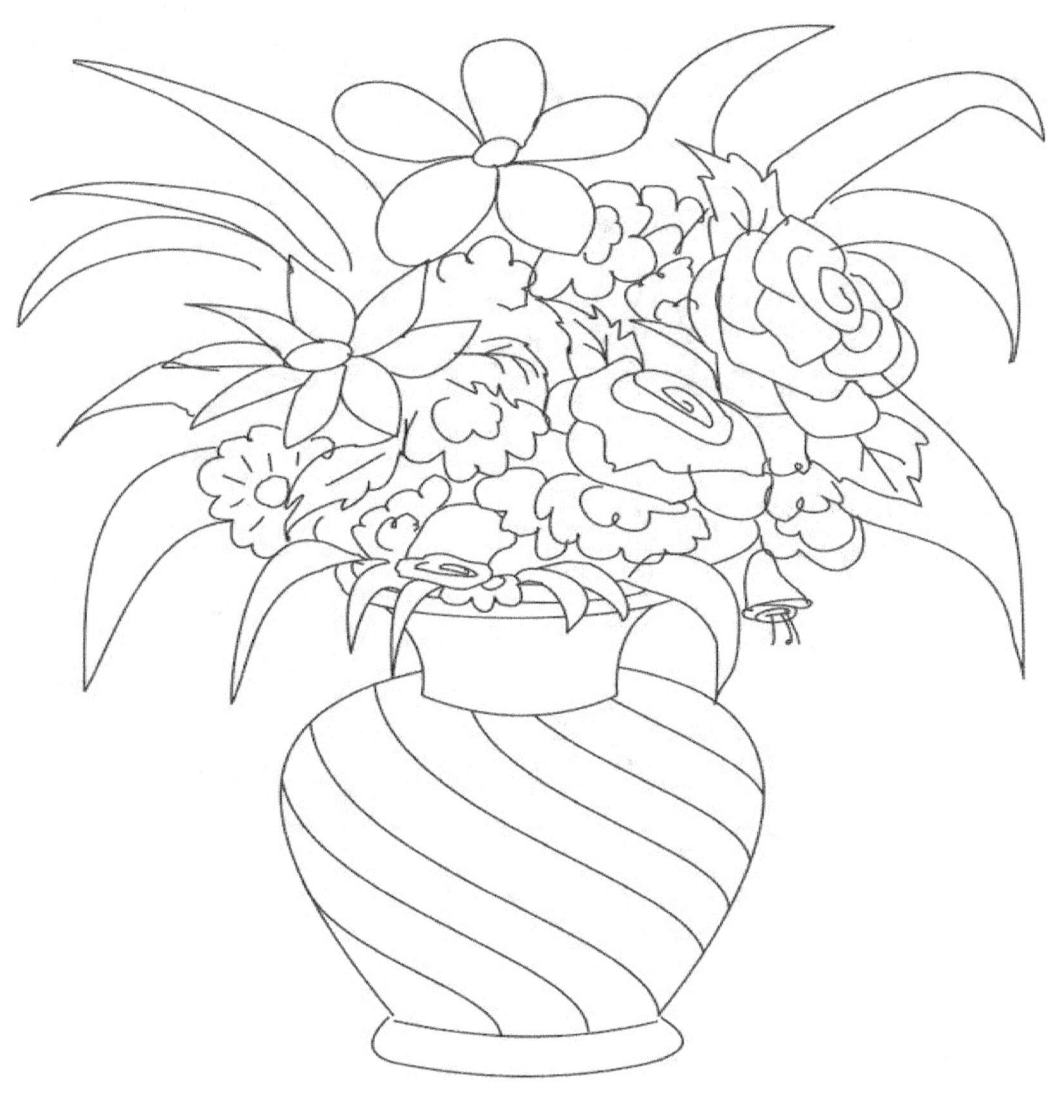

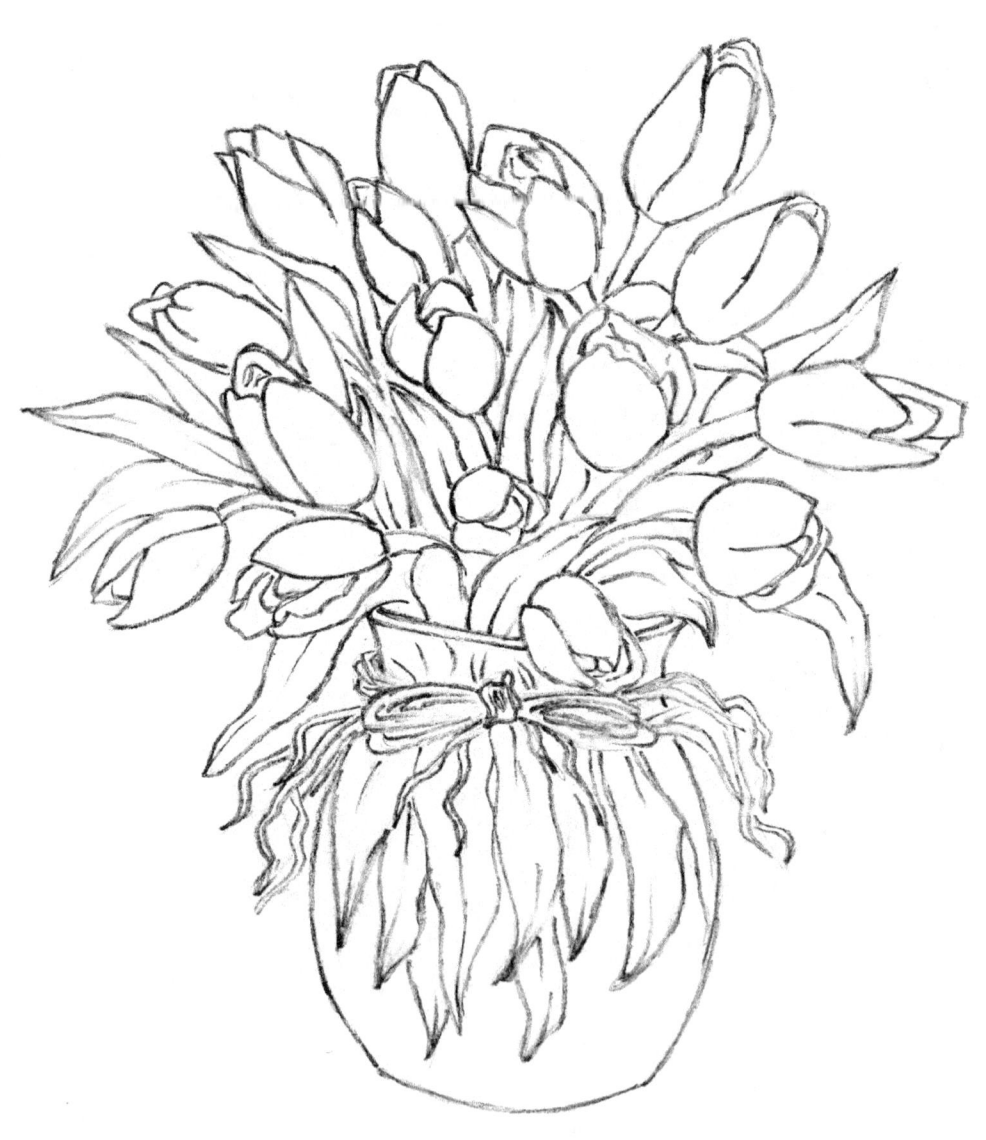

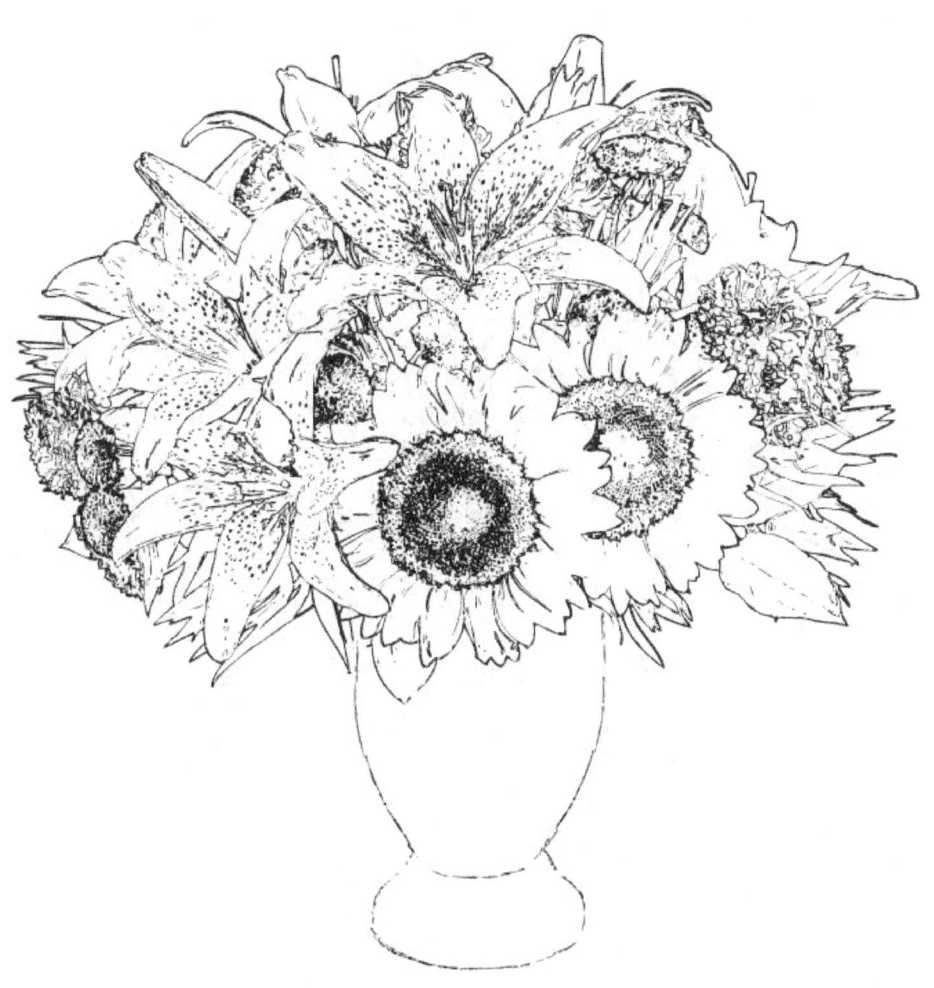

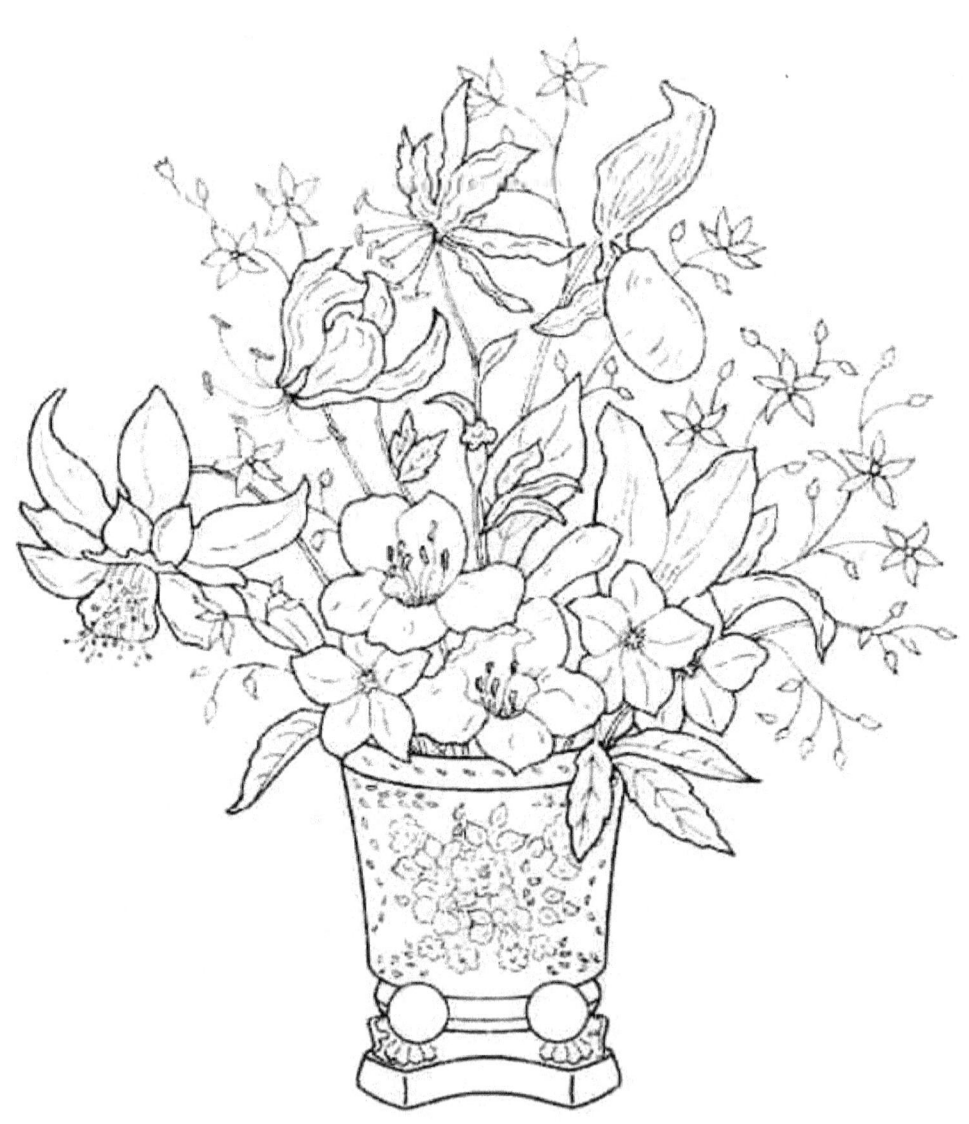

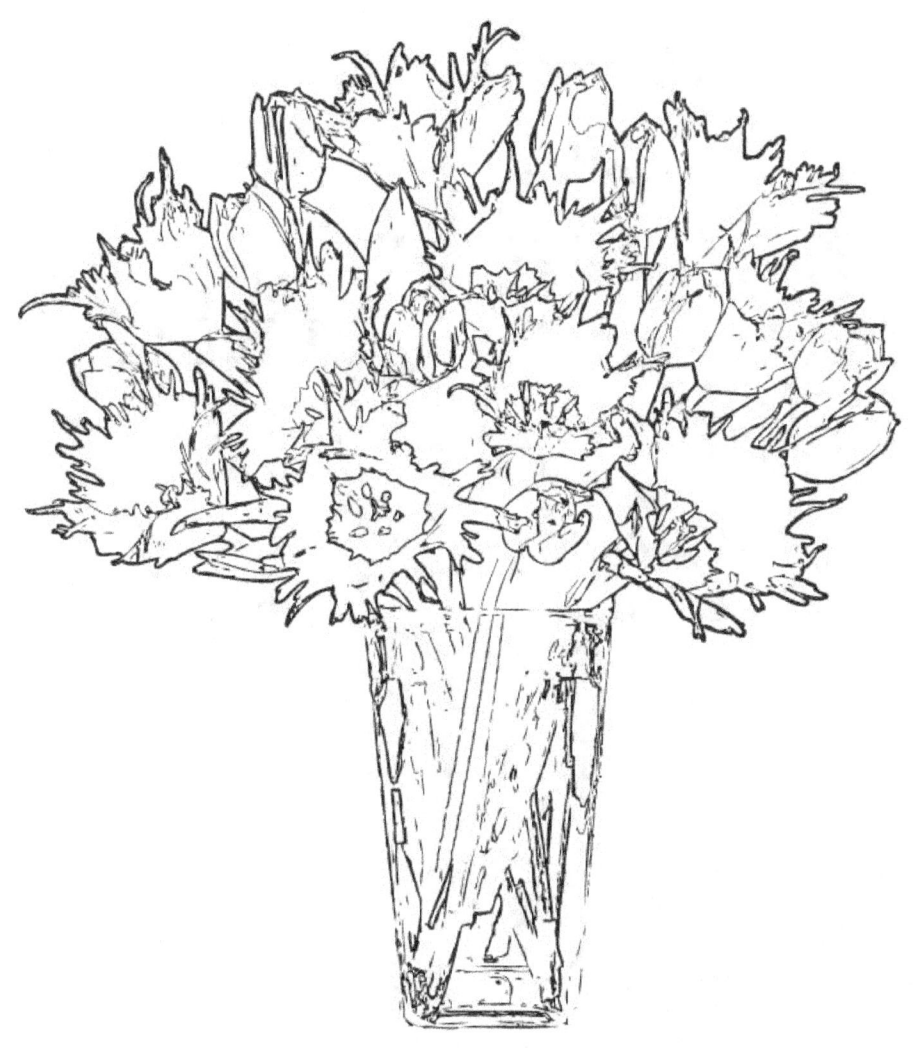

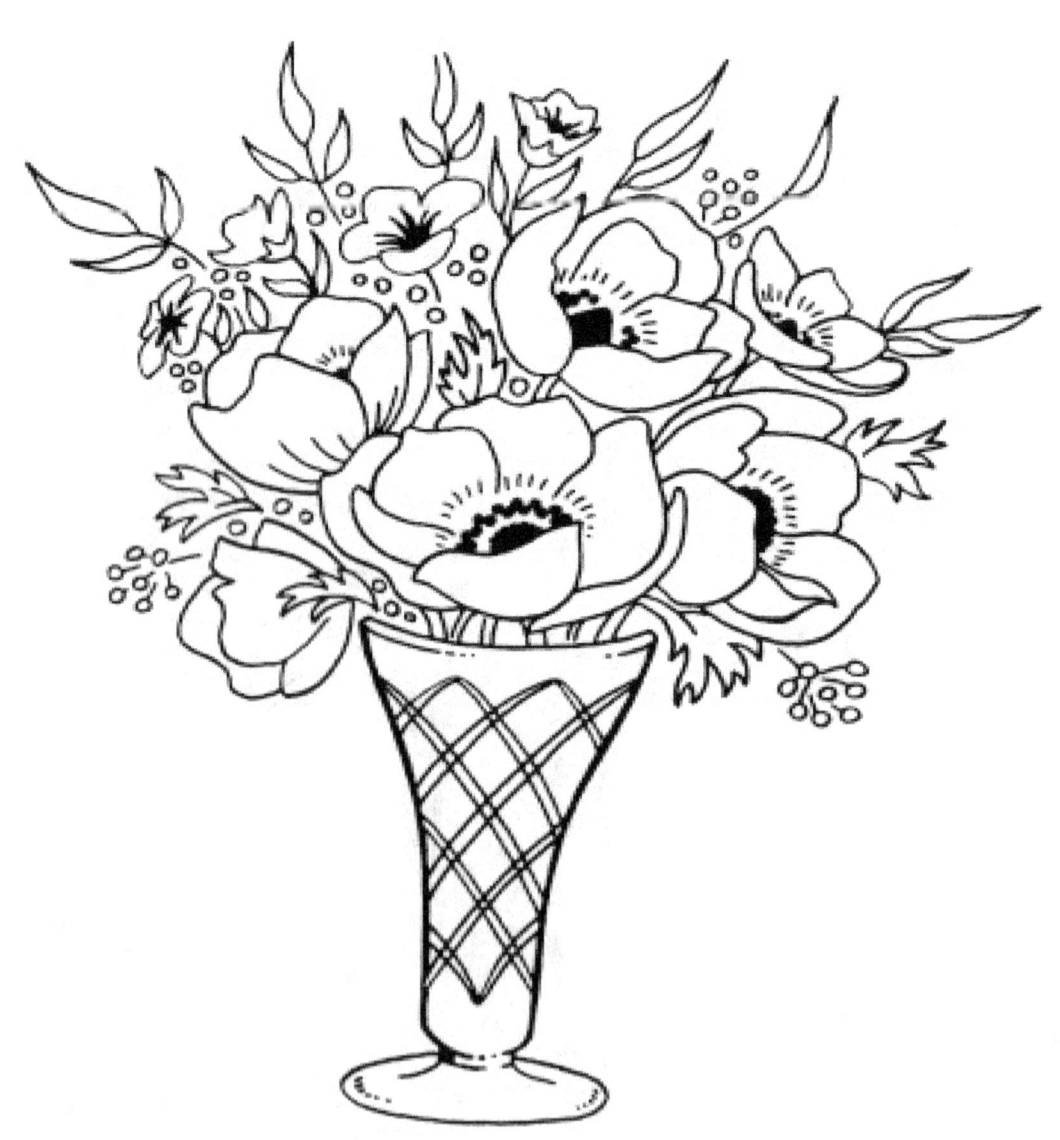

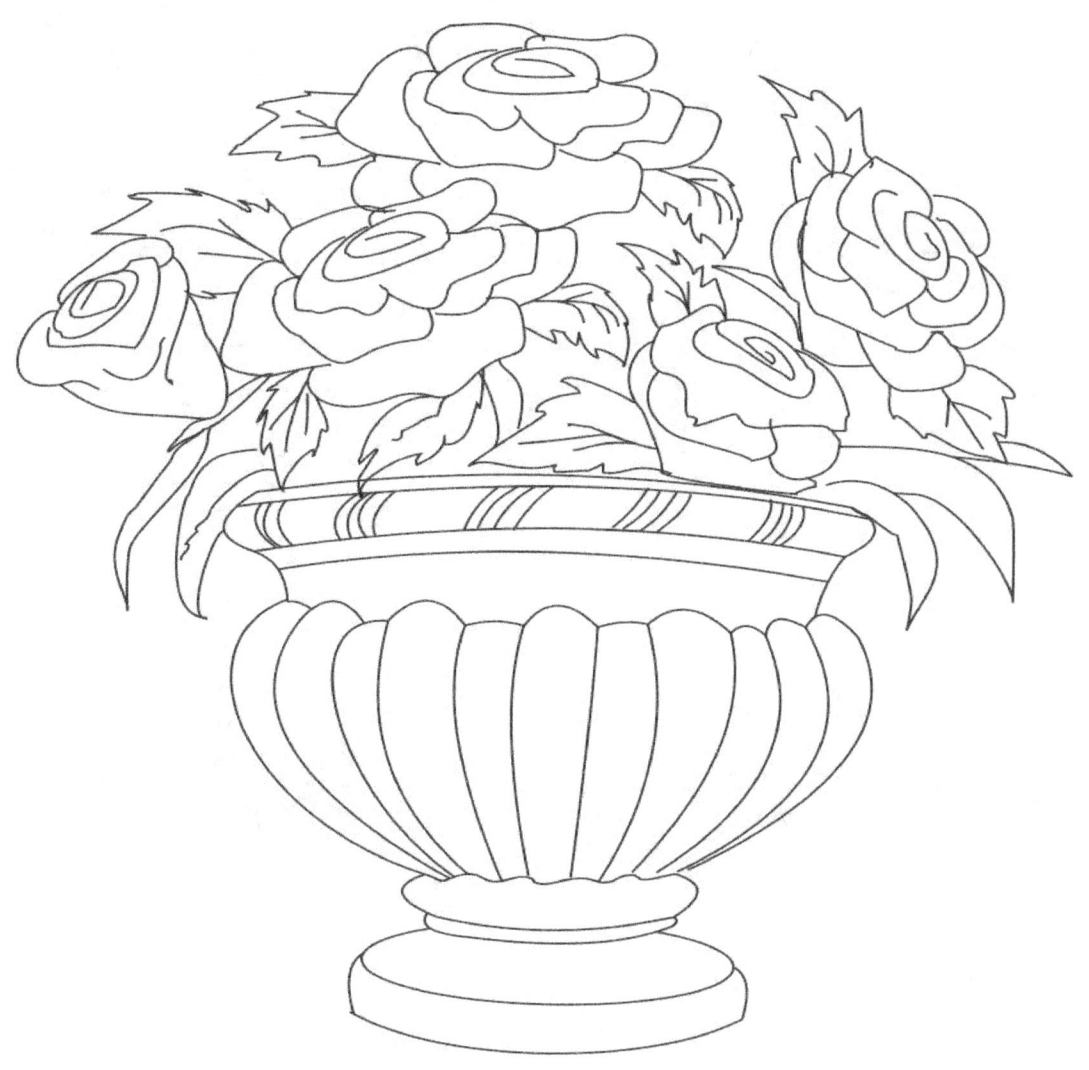

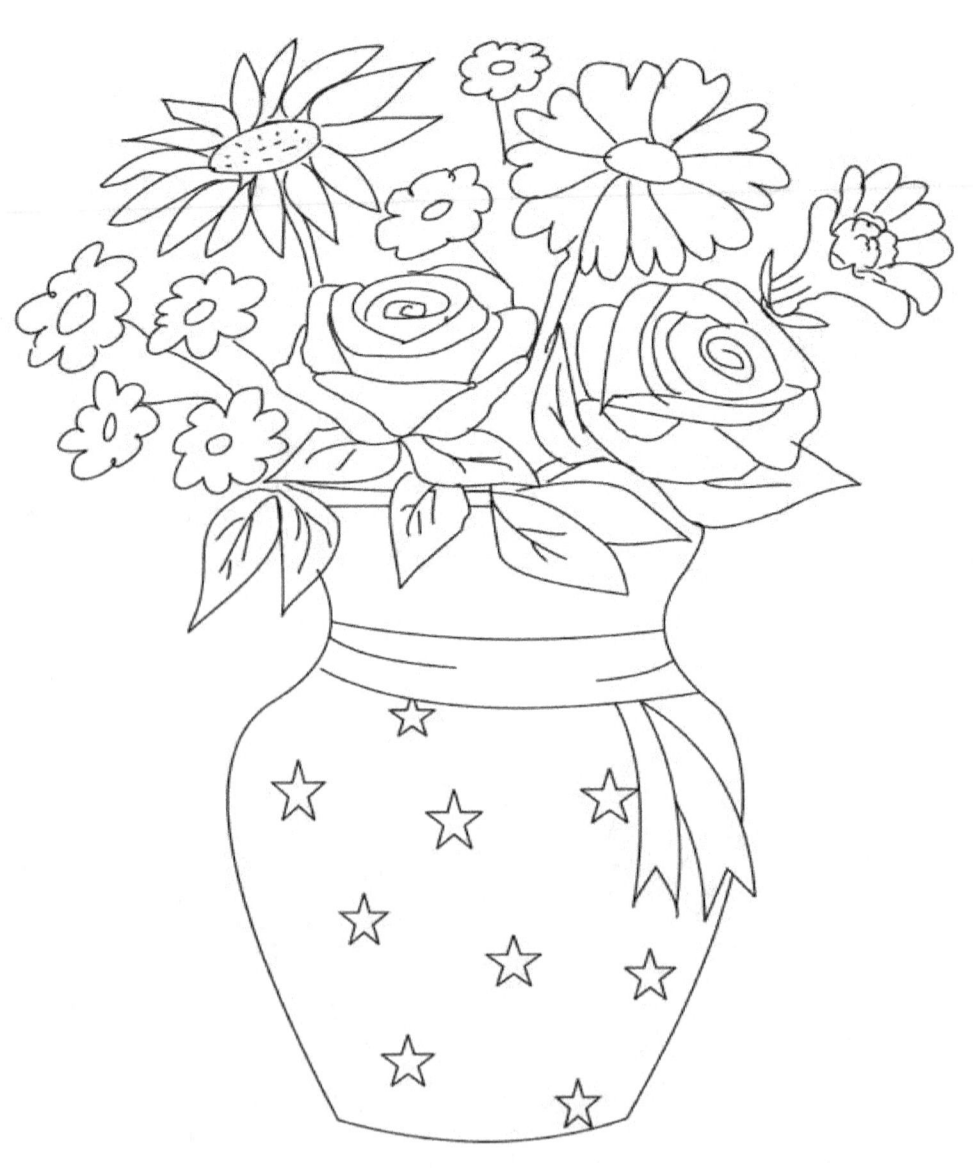

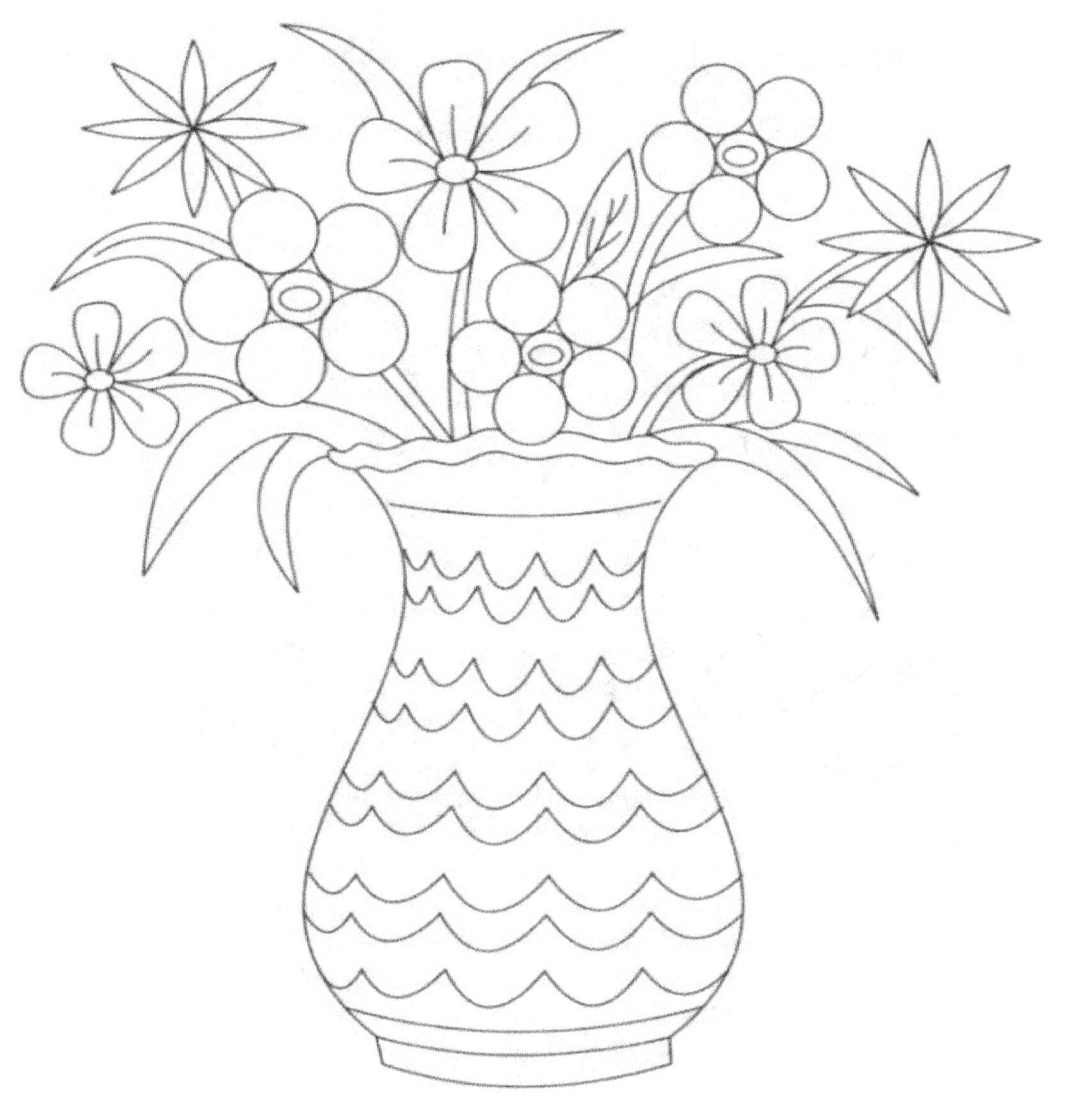

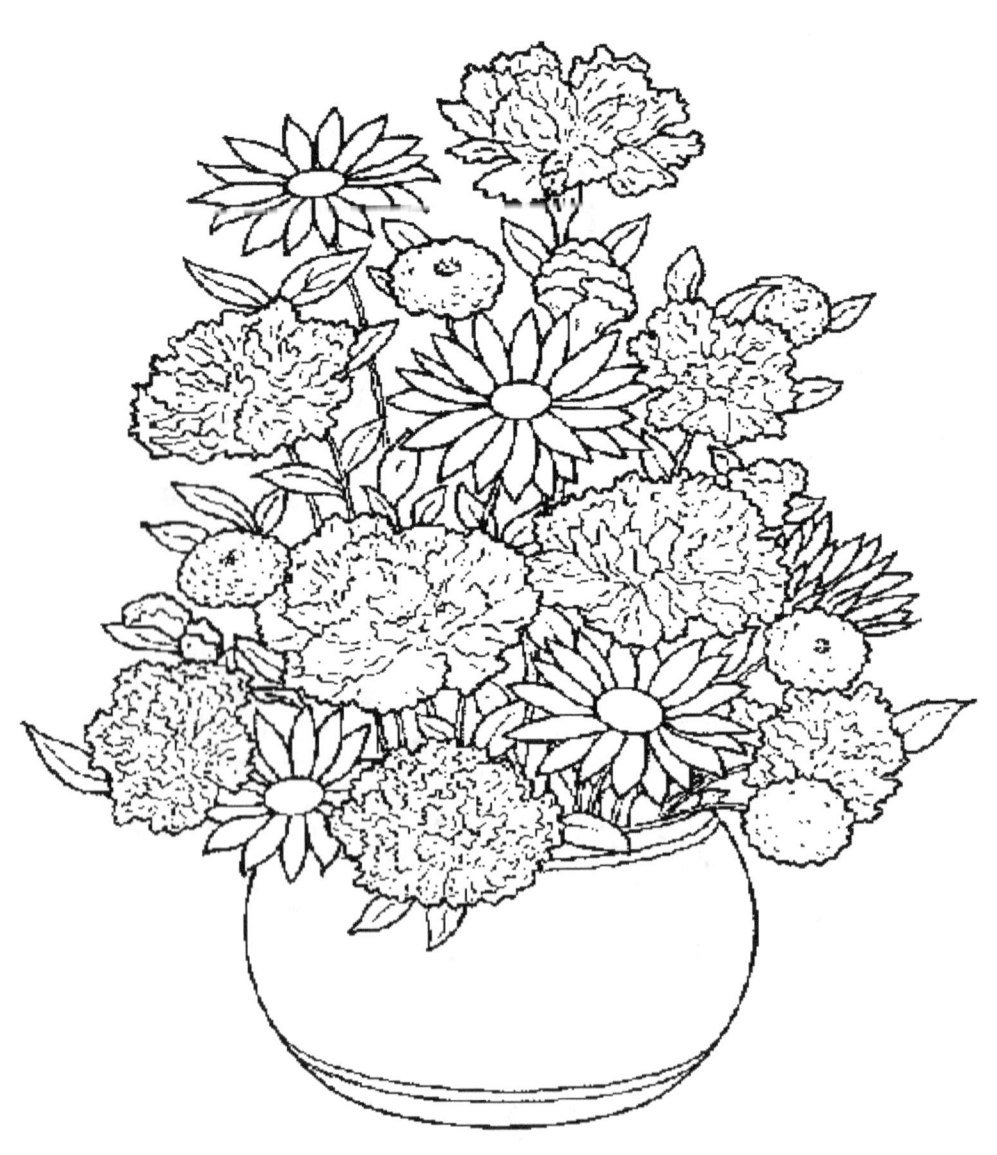

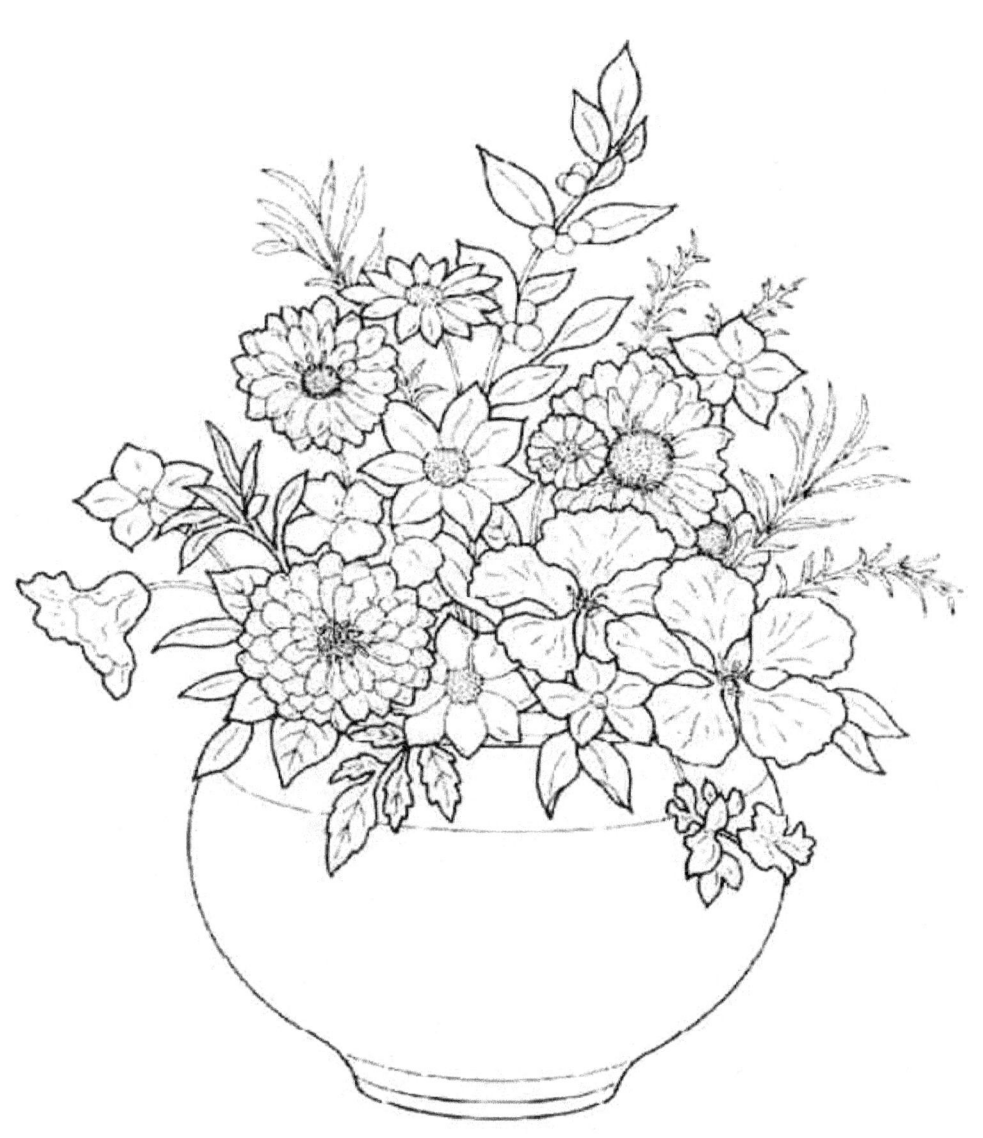

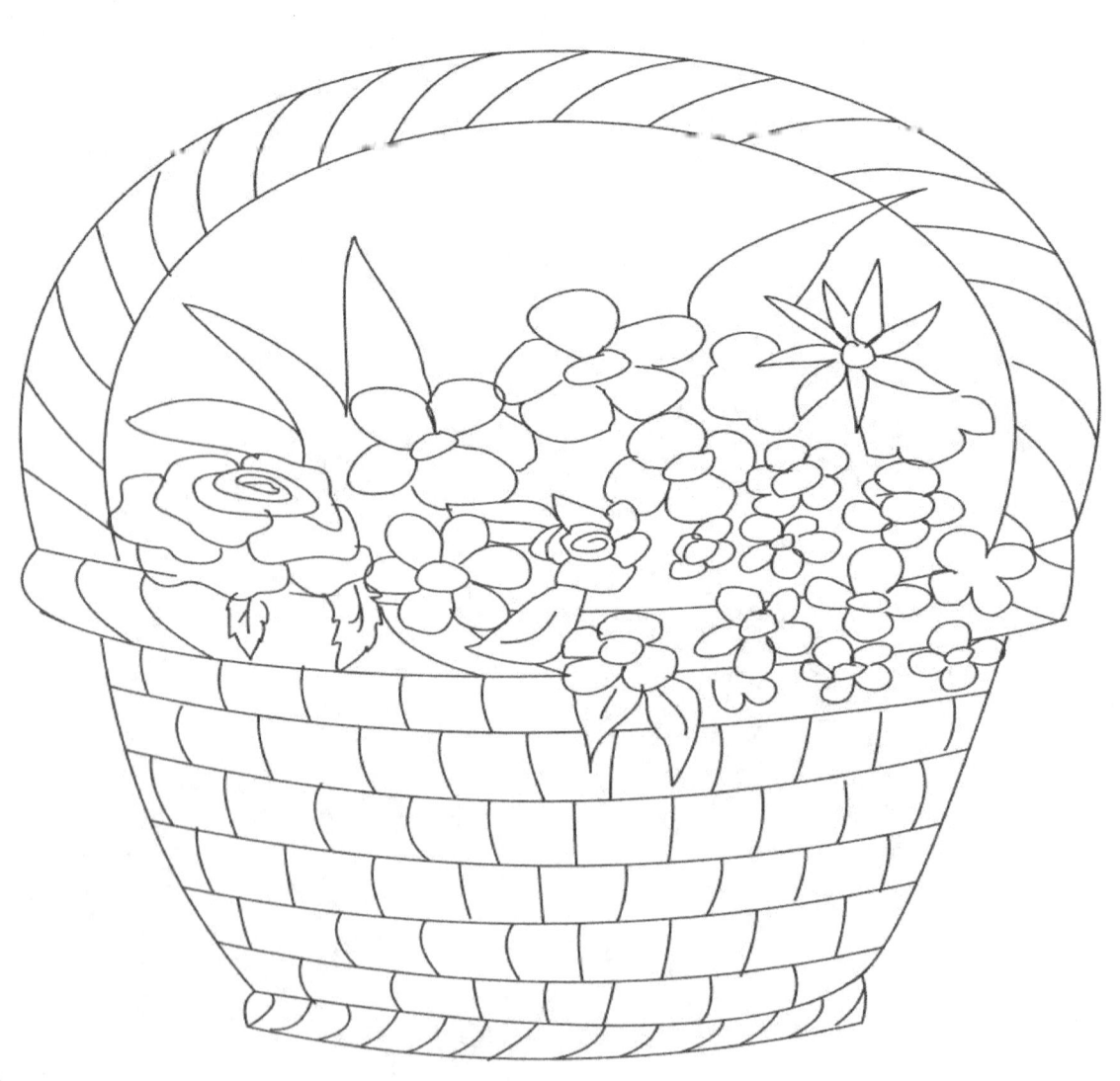

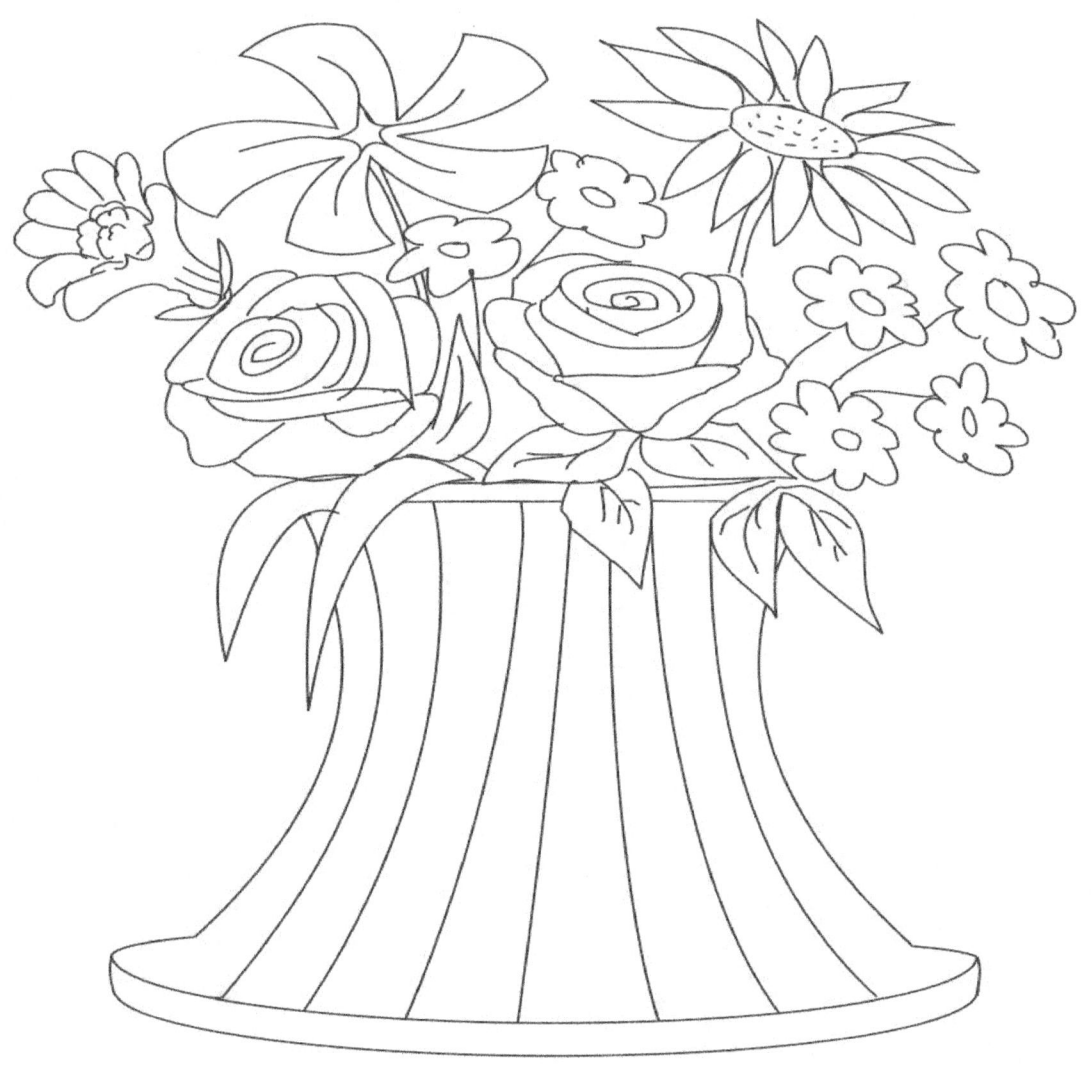

t-compliance